CW01064204

The Days
are Dry

Faye Raye

BookLeaf
Publishing

The Days the Ivies are Dry © 2023 Faye Raye

All rights reserved.

No part of this publication may be reproduced, stored in a retrieval system, or transmitted, in any form or by any means, electronic, mechanical, photocopying, recording or otherwise, without the prior written permission of the presenters.

Faye Raye asserts the moral right to be identified as author of this work.

Presentation by *BookLeaf Publishing*

Web: www.bookleafpub.com

E-mail: info@bookleafpub.com

ISBN: 9789357441810

First edition 2023

For Mum, Maddie and for Ramone.

July Fifteenth

On July fifteenth, sun rises over Siem Reap.
Stagnant water rises to meet a red-less sky
whilst the temple of Angkor, ancient,
emerges, welcomes its ten-thousandth day.

A day that will see the passing of hoards
treading the pre-paraded path
etched out in gap years. Souls
unearthing the already discovered.

Stick prodding at the lily pads resting
from a child, knee-high, on the bank.
Astounded white faces keep distance,
the little one unbothered by ancient wonder.

Though what of mine would captivate her?
Nespresso machine or the Underground.
Fascination at lives not lived, watching
normalcy acted against the backdrop of awe.

On July fifteenth, darkness cocooning the town,
the backstreets of backpacker's paradise
threaten only excitement, the uncertainty.
Of a country still to explore.

A grin wrestles its way, unspoken, as
freedom breathes through my blood.
A certainty rests against exhilaration.
I want to see everything there is.

A Sentence

When I'd imagined loss, time would stop
in a moment of stillness, some calm.
A second to point to in years to come,
my life altered as another was gone.

A Don McLean song of bells ringing,
ceremonious wails in the streets.
A definitive tick, poignant and long
when this life and the next, finally meet.

I thought I'd feel that tectonic shift,
life would no longer be as it was,
yet the timestamp can't be pinpointed
of my small life's greatest loss.

Reality was merely a sentence,
a medic noting no pulse, as a
short life left his body
and the sun came to set on my youth.

The Mould

You're the person who got it-
built worlds through your words,
ones I never asked to be in.
To the day I was sure
I was paradise-bound, chipped
away until I believed.
One tick from discarded,
alone out at sea for a new world
to be built for someone like me.
I fit your mould,
filled in all the holes.
You came along and broke mine.

April Twelfth

There's nothing so sour as
years never to be lived,
ages left untouched
by a life severed too soon.
A mocking day of should-have-
beens, of drinks un-poured
and gifts I'd have bought,
stored away in my head where
I tell myself 'I'll buy them one day'.
There's nothing so sour as
wanting. To celebrate a life
that's already gone.

Dear You

With a skew-whiff fringe, cow-licked apart,
a button nose, always dipped red,
it's your baby blues that draw remarks. Curious,
wide, locked in by crisp lines.

Those eyes that now well at raised voices, at
crowds,
will one day double in size. Pupils expanding
as they lock with another's whilst a
tsunami takes over inside.

They'll blur through nights of excess, strain
to recall all affairs the next day.
They'll bear bruises and stitches from nights,
lost. Even scarred, their mischief will stay.

There will be storms that blaze on so bright
that your baby blues will adjust, the
stillness that comes will become a grey hue,
as chaos overlaps lust.

Those eyes will beg for sleep as three
Screams its arrival each night, but the mind
tapped behind ticks away and away,
scheming to soon take flight.

But, don't let them sting, those eyes will too see
oceans as blue as themselves,
they'll watch swallows race valleys, a blue
whale play,
in a world you don't understand.

In years, your nose will not redden,
your hair will part to the side;
but one thing remains through life's craggy
terrain.
Those eyes will always be mine.

To Be Alive

To feel strangers around, all
insignificant to you, as you to them.
Yet joined momentarily in a crowd.
Tears stinging at poignant words, belted
from fifty-thousand lungs, hearts fused.

Collapsed, unmoving on
these bathroom tiles,
gasping as pain overtakes each
nerve of a heart, shattered.

Dancing with no rhythm, suave, no grace,
we'll sing in any key, at the oldest friend's
wedding. Submit to joy's utter abandon.
The dull throb as disappointment
of fresh failure rests.
Twitching anticipation when
the weed of anger blooms to fume.
Until the sip of early grey begins its healing.

Glancing at the people who love you the most,
who keep you safe in a ruptured world.
Who put up with your indecisiveness,
berate the irrational, mock the moments of ugly.
And celebrate the greatest triumphs

of one, little life.
To look up with a heart full and
know what it is to feel alive.

In These Sheets

His chest falls quicker than it rises,
small puffs of air with each drop, as
a thumb strokes mine whilst sleep takes his eyes
but mine still bore holes in the ceiling.
Though I am safe in these sheets that I bought,
laid next to a heart that loves mine, I'll still
gasp for breath in this room, its air thinning
as tight panic takes over inside.

I'll fight off the thought of past bruises, of spats
with those who showed care by force,
think now of the pride in my freckled-man's
eyes
of the kindness behind every thought.
Whilst he sleeps, I'll just use my own voice
to reassure that I'm safe in these sheets.
To drown out the panic that creeps to my bed,
left by men whose love could impede.

Every Four Years

She'll watch each drip drop of Stella
leave the pint and foam-coat his lips
that shout obscenities at France
on a losing English pitch.
Pray this one will be his last whilst
light drains from frosting eyes
until she'll take herself to bed too soon,
their routine of each four years.
Now screwed shut, pretend to sleep
as he fumbles from his jeans.
Just wait the night out 'til morning
hope ice thaws, hope spite leaves.

Forget Me (not)

Each summer I head,
where Mom lived to twenty.
We drive her old stomping ground as she
regales tales I could recite word-for-word.

The Mecca Hall where Nan worked, with its
railings Mom swung from whilst waiting.
She'll point out her first home, humble and
worn.
'I remember it being further uphill'. Every
single year.

We'll get to an island where traffic is teeming,
stone-faced she'll nod, to a pub near the road.
'Your Grandad would leave us with cokes
outside
whilst he drank until late every evening'.

She'll say, 'It's like someone else's life'
with a fondness so rife,
yet tears sting her eyes.

The Peas

A friend still tells me about the peas
that slid down her mum's dry-cleaned dress.
On the doorframe, hanging in plastic,
iron-pressed to soon make its debut.
When her father came home, tore
the cloth from the table, ripping dinner
to the living room floor.
Gravy and peas slid down the cold plastic.

At five years old, she watched the peas race,
too afraid to look back up. Relief washing over
that the dress was not ruined; that something,
at least, had protection.

In a Youth Spent

I've my sister beside me.
She boasts better driver.
We hum our same voices
yet her lisp is slight. Omitting
the same lines that blast through the aux,
laughter ringing large as our
Sisterly Sense is declared.

Freedom of a youth spent in a Mini,
time freezing each tradition's time.
Zeppelin and Lionel that dad raised us on.
Mixtapes from who-knows;
long-losts now score our bond.

The sand's warmth mourns another sunset
missed,
planned without caution, the sea's cavity calling.
'Remember when we…' roared over Fleetwood.
Familiar roads absorb secrets we howl.

A tradition constant as her in my world,
albums that healed lives halved, shared. Lost.
Once we're really grown, mum's spare rooms
repurposed, it's singing in a Mini,
I'll miss the most.

Nannerl

A prodigy they'd say, beyond her years.
Scribbling scores to hand to her brother.
Shipped off around Europe, a child
to marvel with hands made to
craft symphonies. Ignite flames
in the stiffest of Western elite,
hypnotise them with child's divine gift.
A reputation that stretches beyond
adolescence. Encapsulates expertise.
Now you go and get married, sew
blankets for babes as Amadeus
becomes who he will.
Absence of a womb leaving
room
for chance. Whilst this man's
wife remains still.
She'll sit idly by, allow skill
so inherent to flourish
to glory, renown.
The name she once donned to
expand, be exalted, its eminence
tied to honour mankind.
An option too male for this prodigy
left, in her motherhood, behind.

Vemödalen

There are albums in phones
across the wide globe
that capture the worlds
greatest gifts. The same shots,
non-unique.

Snaps of the view
from Machu Picchu,
Trocadero frame of the tower.
A million Mona Lisas,
of holding up Pisas.
Big Buddhas and Ha Giang loops.

Though yours, his and mine
catch new moments in time.
A new Earth from the one last week.
Tomorrow, new photos in cities, changed.
The world as it sits,
Before time rewrites once more.

Only Loss

Our street seemed longer at seven years old,
young eyes heavy from the day's spelling test.
Mum's key still left in the lock when she ran
upstairs, toward the hissing.
I'd never before heard water hiss.
It cascaded through stories, to my soggy socks.
Panic thick in her voice as she yelled from above
'Check the kitchen. Now'. The ceiling caved in
as
dilated pupils witnessed our home
crumbling from within, only
to remain a cold shell for months to come.

A guilt bubbled low down, uncertainty
surrounding who to blame.

One evening I had tea at a friend's house,
hers remaining as we'd always known.
I was jealous of the carpet.
Our floor, sanded to a shine in places whilst
others were left rough, made me itch.
I would jump to each shiny spot,
steppingstones through lava.
There was nostalgia for how it once was,
I'd never before lost anything.

I don't recall any fear,
as a child amidst a flood.
Only loss.

And Yet the Room Fills

Glasses clink and cheers are mumbled
amongst live-in strangers, curiosity rife.
Water waits at the door.

Dancing, flirting and
shouldn't-have-done-thats
follow card games, tally charts
and beer-sodden beer mats.
Afternoon debates heat over
MPs. Who's best to stand?
'You wouldn't understand'.
Drunken proclamations of friendship.
Of gratitude.
As the room begins to fill.

Midday sun beats on a beach-
we'll escape the Welsh winter
but the water still seeps.
Icebox passed around person-to-person.
Lost phones, keys, credit cards, weed.
Cheap drinks split down us and
who's best at pulling?
Frail promises of friendship.
Of love.
And yet, the room fills.

Until lies and mistakes
replace film nights.
Side-picking spat through
green-venomed words.
As the cogs of friendship
rust over.
There's too much water.

Glasses break,
pointed fingers accuse.
'Your true colours are showing'.
Drowning, still kicking.
Just stay afloat
as lungs overflow and power
diminishes. The fallen friend.
No goodbyes, few tears shed.
The water begins to drain.

Left with just voices, visceral,
memory never fading with time.
Etched into my thoughts and carried through
life.
Bitter with anger, stifled with fear.
Saddened by the rose-tinted echo of
glasses clinking.

The drowning subsides.
I look up, and the room is empty.

Saviour

Losing hope, choleric faces, tightened jaws.
Losing the plans, homes and the destinations.
Losing years of a life, never coming to fruition.
A future that will never hold.

To regain freedom, the self recognised in a
mirror.
To regain dignity, pride to speak with a whole
voice.
To regain sight of who still stands in the rubble.
For preservation.

To lose the version once was, to save what is
true.

November Nineteenth

I lie on a rooftop, a stone
in my side, the concrete pillow
has only now cooled.
Breathing in unison with friends
to each side, as galaxies ripple.
Shift, to never go back. A star dies
as it paints the sky, earning
gasps that never grow old.
A meteor shower whilst
doused in love. We'll all soon
shift with the Milky way.
But for now,
I'll stay.

Home

There's a bed I know will always be made
when I return from the heaviest days.
A cushion she's fluffed up just because
before she potters around in her house,
furniture that shifts subtly, nearly unnoticed.
'Do you want tea?'.
The bathroom transformed to the Amazon
on the days the ivies are dry.
'Faye the telly's not working!' -
it wasn't switched on.
Post-its of love you's left next to the kettle,
curled up with the cat every night.
A house that she'll heat
though she's comfy already,
cheesecake she'll bake to relieve.
In a little oasis, no matter how far.
Home is always my mum.

Jump

Nothing is saying 'no' so
why should I? My pulse may
soar, but it will again fall
and I won't have to wonder.
If fear is a gauge then
the highs could be more.
There's too much to do
to let weeds wrap around
my ankles that seek out white sand.
And if all goes wrong, I'll try
twice more. I've never before
fallen once and for all…

Branched

At twenty-five, before you can drive
your best friend will walk down the aisle.
Whilst you scour the net for budget flights,
she'll choose new shelves for the hall.
She'll miscarry the baby they'd tried for all year
the same week you try out the coil.
When the tears on your cheeks have pride
woven
in, as you think of the men you've cut clean,
plucking the courage to choose a new life,
she'll settle into her married routine.

She'll climb the steps of a corporate ladder,
driving a car you will never afford,
as life takes you from jobless to jobs,
fund the insatiable will to explore.
When she's at her desk, you'll climb mountains,
all the Wonders in one short year.
She'll go home to husband, dogs, and hot
dinners
whilst you search for the cheapest beer.
Visit countries she found out existed
from the pub quiz at Ye Olde Shakespeare.

By thirty, she'll rent out her first house

to tenants much younger than you.
You'll have watched the sun set through
thousands of eyes, red skies through tasteless
wine,
as she and hubby make a taster menu
to impress her boss's new wife.
You'll meet her for coffee, regale the tales
of your life on a twisting dirt road,
She'll gush about mister, the dogs, and their
homes,
knowing her river still flows beside yours.

A Life Philosophy

I used to hear 'amen' and feel
I was missing, somewhere,
a sixth sense.
That I see no god, no after or plan
so, my life somehow must lack reason.
It is in the nothingness that I find my hope,
that nothing matters, not me,
so, my slips do not last,
my glories will pass. And I am left
with a life to enjoy.

To just be.

Milton Keynes UK
Ingram Content Group UK Ltd.
UKHW020735030823
426269UK00015B/687